1

FRENCH VERBS
made *EASY*
plus

Rosemary Pitts, M.A.

Third Edition August 2021

© 2019, 2020, 2021 Rosemary Pitts

All rights reserved. No part of this publication may be reproduced, stored in any retrieval system, or transmitted in any form or by any means, electronic, mechanical, photocopying, recording, or otherwise, without the prior permission of the copyright owner.

Contents

Preface & Foreword to the Third Edition   4

FRENCH VERBS made EASY   5

PRESENT – l'indicatif présent   6
You = tu or vous?   7
Regular –ER Verbs   8
Regular –IR Verbs   12
Regular –RE Verbs   13
Irregular –ER Verbs   14

IRREGULAR VERBS   18

avoir être aller boire   19
conduire connaître courir devoir   20
dire écrire faire lire   21
mettre ouvrir pouvoir prendre   22
recevoir savoir sortir venir   23
voir vouloir (suivre craindre)   24

Reflexive verbs – verbes pronominaux   25
PERFECT – passé composé – verbs conjugated with avoir   26
Agreement of the past participle (with avoir)   30
PERFECT – passé composé – verbs conjugated with être   31
Agreement of the past participle (with être)   31
IMPERFECT – imparfait   34
FUTURE – futur simple   36
CONDITIONAL – conditionnel   38
PLUPERFECT – plus-que-parfait   39
PAST HISTORIC – passé simple   41
When to use which tense   44
NEGATIVES – le négatif   48
QUESTIONS – questions   51

3

plus GRAMMAR TIPS 54

Le La Les 55
Useful questions 58
Opinions 59
Stressed Pronouns 61
à 63
de 65
du, de la, des 67
Adjectives – les adjectifs 69
- Useful Regular Adjectives 70
- Adjectives ending in 'e' 71
- Irregular adjectives 73

Object Pronouns 78
Special Structures/Idioms etc. 83
- c'est 84
- il y a 85
- avoir 15 ans 86
- devoir / il faut 87
- ça me plaît 88
- si 88
- depuis 89
- être 90
- venir de 90
- savoir/connaître 90
- Verbs with no preposition 91

Topic Vocabulary 92
- Numbers – Numéros 92
- Days – Jours 94
- Months and Seasons – Mois et Saisons 95
- The Time – L'Heure 96
- The Weather – La Météo 97
- Towns – Villes 99
- Countries – Pays 100
- Sport – Sport 102
- Music – Musique 104

Vocabulary Tips 105

Preface

Having trouble getting your head round FRENCH VERBS?
They aren't as difficult as you may think.

This brightly coloured book, with its accompanying set of YouTube videos, is designed to be the perfect desk companion for any teacher of French, or beginner, KS3 or GCSE student. The whole French verb system is boiled down to its simplest components, to make it as easy as possible to understand and memorise.

The basic philosophy is to explain in visual terms what happens to individual verbs or groups of verbs, as a teacher would explain it. Recurring patterns are made crystal-clear. The stems of verbs are carefully lined up so that you can easily follow the changes that occur. Different colours immediately highlight patterns. Tricky irregularities and important variations are marked in a range of colours, bold type, italics, capital letters and underlining. You can quickly see the main groups of verbs and you will learn how easy it is to form different tenses and when to use them.

The rationale behind this method of setting out verbs was born of the author's six decades of experience teaching French in school classrooms and in one-to-one tutoring.

The whole book has been recorded in a series of videos – like short lessons, with correct pronunciation and spellings read out. Search for "Rosemary's French Verbs Made Easy" on YouTube.

Foreword to the Third Edition

This third edition contains a section of **Grammar Tips**. This is not a comprehensive outline of French Grammar. Your text book should provide that. This section is intended to clarify points of grammar and vocabulary which are commonly misunderstood.

Examples contain a range of useful everyday vocabulary.

Also now available – as a paperback (or freely downloadable pdf) – is a Workbook which contains practice sentences designed to help you master the verbs laid out in this book.

5

FRENCH VERBS made *EASY*

Verbs are DOING words. We use them all the time to explain what is happening – or what HAS happened or WILL happen.

The vast majority of French verbs all work in the same way – so they are called REGULAR.

Eg: PARLER = to speak

We start with the PRESENT tense to indicate what we are doing now or what we usually do.

PRESENT – l'indicatif présent

You need six persons for each verb:

SINGULAR

je = I

tu = you (singular)

il = he (or it masculine)   The **il** form is also used for
- **elle** = she / it (feminine)
- **on** = one / we
- Any ONE person or thing

Eg: Pierre, le boulanger, ma mère, Marie, le chat, l'enfant, la maison.

PLURAL

nous = we

vous = you (plural or polite singular)

ils = they   The **ils** form is also used for
- **elles** = they (feminine)
- Any group of persons or things

Eg: mes parents, Olivier et Chantal, les garçons, les livres, mes sœurs.

7

You = tu or vous?

Use the tu form to address a family member, a friend, a child, or an animal.

Use the vous form to address TWO or more people.

vous is also a polite form of addressing any ONE adult unless family.

Eg: shop assistant, teacher, fireman

Regular –ER Verbs

There are thousands of verbs which follow this pattern. New verbs usually follow it too.

Eg: surfer, stopper, cliquer, interviewer

The **INFINITIVE** of these verbs ends in **-ER**.

The **INFINITIVE** is the form of the verb which is not attached to a subject – je, tu, etc.

parler = to speak		
je	parle =	*I speak, I am speaking, I do speak*
tu	parles	
il	parle	
nous	parlons	
vous	parlez	
ils	parlent	

NOTE: The endings in green are SILENT.

Verbs beginning with a vowel or "h" – **je** ➔ **j'**

aimer = to like / love	
j'	aime = I like / love
tu	aimes
il	aime
nous	aim**ons**
vous	aim**ez**
ils	aiment

On the next two pages there is a list of common -**ER** verbs for you to practise. There are several thousand more!

accompagn**er**	to accompany		dans**er**	to dance
achet**er**	to buy (see p.16)		demand**er**	to ask (for)
aid**er**	to help		dépens**er**	to spend (money)
aim**er**	to like		désir**er**	to desire
ajout**er**	to add		dessin**er**	to draw
allum**er**	to light		détest**er**	to hate
apport**er**	to bring		devin**er**	to guess
* arriv**er**	to arrive		discut**er**	to argue
attach**er**	to attach		distribu**er**	to distribute
attrap**er**	to catch		donn**er**	to give
bavard**er**	to chat		dur**er**	to last
boug**er**	to move (see p.17)		écout**er**	to listen (to)
cach**er**	to hide		emprunt**er**	to borrow
cass**er**	to break		* entr**er**	to enter / go in
chant**er**	to sing		examin**er**	to examine
cherch**er**	to seek / look for		expliqu**er**	to explain
collectionn**er**	to collect		ferm**er**	to shut
command**er**	to order		frapp**er**	to hit
commenc**er**	to start / begin (p.17)		fum**er**	to smoke
compt**er**	to count		gagn**er**	to win / gain / earn
continu**er**	to continue		gard**er**	to keep
coup**er**	to cut		grimp**er**	to climb
coût**er**	to cost		grogn**er**	to grumble

habit**er**	to live
invit**er**	to invite
jou**er**	to play
laiss**er**	to let / leave
lav**er**	to wash
lou**er**	to hire / praise
mang**er**	to eat ^(see p.17)
march**er**	to walk
* mont**er**	to climb / go up
montr**er**	to show
nag**er**	to swim ^(see p.17)
organis**er**	to organise
ôt**er**	to take off (clothes)
oubli**er**	to forget
parl**er**	to talk / speak
pass**er**	to pass
pay**er**	to pay (for) ^(see p.15)
pêch**er**	to fish
pens**er**	to think
pleur**er**	to cry
port**er**	to carry / wear
pos**er**	to put
pouss**er**	to push

prépar**er**	to prepare
quitt**er**	to leave
racont**er**	to tell / relate
ramass**er**	to pick up
regard**er**	to watch / look (at)
remarqu**er**	to notice
remerci**er**	to thank
rencontr**er**	to meet
répar**er**	to repair
* rest**er**	to stay / remain
sembl**er**	to seem
souffl**er**	to blow
téléphon**er**	to phone
tir**er**	to pull
* tomb**er**	to fall
touch**er**	to touch
travaill**er**	to work
travers**er**	to cross
trembl**er**	to tremble
trouv**er**	to find
vérifi**er**	to verify / check
voyag**er**	to travel ^(see p.17)

* *conjugated with* **être** *in* **passé composé**

There are 2 much smaller groups of REGULAR VERBS: **–IR** verbs and **-RE** verbs.

Regular –IR Verbs

finir = to finish	
je	finis = *I finish / end, I am finishing, I do finish*
tu	finis
il	finit
nous	finissons
vous	finissez
ils	finissent

The following **-IR** verbs follow the above pattern:

applaudir	to applaud		**rempl**ir	to fill
avertir	to notify / warn		**réuss**ir	to succeed
choisir	to choose		**roug**ir	to turn red / blush
réfléchir	to reflect		**sais**ir	to seize / grab

Regular –RE Verbs

vendre = to sell		

je	vends =	*I sell*
		I am selling
		I do sell
tu	vends	
il	vend	
nous	vendons	
vous	vendez	
ils	vendent	

The following -**RE** verbs follow the above pattern:

attendre	to wait (for)
* **descendre**	to go down
entendre	to hear
perdre	to lose
répondre	to reply / answer

* *conjugated with **être** in **passé composé.** See p.32*

Once you have learned these regular verbs you have **mastered most French verbs.**

> Pages 14-17 contain details you can study later. You may prefer to go straight to the VERY IMPORTANT IRREGULAR VERBS on PAGE 18.

Some **-ER** verbs are **slightly irregular** in parts.

A. The following changes occur before the SILENT "**e**" in the je, tu, il and ils forms. So they are sometimes referred to as the **1, 2, 3 and 6 verbs**.

1) l ➜ ll

appeler = to call

1	j'	appell**e** = I call / am calling
2	tu	appell**es**
3	il	appell**e**
4	nous	appel**ons**
5	vous	appel**ez**
6	ils	appell**ent**

ALSO:

* s'appeler	to be called
rappeler	to recall
* se rappeler	to remember

Reflexive. See page 25

2) t ➔ tt

jeter = to throw

je	jette = I throw / am throwing / do throw
tu	jettes
il	jette
nous	jetons
vous	jetez
ils	jettent

3) -ayer / -oyer / -uyer   y ➔ i

essayer = to try

j'	essaie = I try / am trying / do try
tu	essaies
il	essaie
nous	essayons
vous	essayez
ils	essaient

ALSO:

aboyer	to bark
* s'ennuyer	to be bored
nettoyer	to clean
payer	to pay

4) e ➔ è

acheter = to buy / purchase

j'	ach**è**te = I buy / am buying / do buy
tu	ach**è**tes
il	ach**è**te
nous	achetons
vous	achetez
ils	ach**è**tent

ALSO:

* se lever	to get up
mener	to lead
amener	to bring
emmener	to take away
* se promener	to walk

5) é ➔ è

espérer = to hope

j'	esp**è**re = I hope / am hoping / do hope
tu	esp**è**res
il	esp**è**re
nous	espérons
vous	espérez
ils	esp**è**rent

ALSO:

compléter	to complete
* s'inquiéter	to worry
préférer	to prefer
répéter	to repeat

Reflexive. See page 25

B. The following changes occur before **a, o, u**.

1) g → ge

manger = to eat		
je	mange = I eat / am eating / do eat	
tu	manges	
il	mange	
nous	mangeons	
vous	mangez	
ils	mangent	

ALSO:

bouger	to move
changer	to change
interroger	to question
nager	to swim
neiger	to snow
ranger	to tidy away
voyager	to travel

2) c → ç

commencer = to start / begin		
je	commence = I start / am starting / do start	
tu	commences	
il	commence	
nous	commençons	
vous	commencez	
ils	commencent	

ALSO:

annoncer	to announce
avancer	to advance
lancer	to throw

18

IRREGULAR VERBS

Some verbs do NOT fit into these patterns. A number of common verbs are IRREGULAR - probably because they are so frequently used that they have become worn out!

We could not get through even a brief conversation without using words like "can", "go", "must", "am", "has", "is", "put".

The most common IRREGULAR VERBS are set out here.
It is worth noting the following exceptions:

1. All **"nous"** forms end in **"-ons"**
   except **nous SOMMES** (from **être**)

2. All **"vous"** forms end in **"-ez"**
   except **vous ÊTES** (from **être**)
   vous DITES (from **dire**)
   vous FAITES (from **faire**)

3. All **"ils"** forms end in SILENT **"-ent"**
   Except **ils ONT** (from **avoir**)
   ils SONT (from **être**)
   ils FONT (from **faire**)
   ils VONT (from **aller**)

Please note that the coloured letters, **bold type** and *italics* in this section are designed to help you see and remember the tricky bits. You will spot that the je, tu and il forms often end in –s,-s,-t or –x,-x,-t and that the nous and vous forms are often the odd ones out.

*av*oir = to have

j'	**ai**	I have
tu	as	you have
il	a	he has
nous	*av*ons	we have
vous	*av*ez	you have
ils	**ont**	they have

être = to be

je	**suis**	I am
tu	es	you are
il	est	he is
nous	**sommes**	we are
vous	**êtes**	you are
ils	**sont**	they are

*all*er = to go

je	**v**ais	= I go / am going / do go
tu	**v**as	
il	**v**a	
nous	*all*ons	
vous	*all*ez	
ils	**v**ont	

boire = to drink

je	bois	= I drink / etc.
tu	bois	
il	boit	
nous	***bu*v**ons	
vous	***bu*v**ez	
ils	boi**v**ent	

conduire = to lead / drive

je	conduis = I lead
tu	conduis
il	conduit
nous	conduisons
vous	conduisez
ils	conduisent

ALSO:

déduire	to deduce
produire	to produce
traduire	to translate
construire	to build / construct
détruire	to destroy

connaître = to know (a person or place)

je	connais = I know
tu	connais
il	connaît
nous	connaissons
vous	connaissez
ils	connaissent

ALSO:

reconnaître	to recognize
paraître	to appear / seem
apparaître	to appear / to put in an appearance
disparaître	to disappear

courir = to run

je	cours = I run
tu	cours
il	court
nous	courons
vous	courez
ils	courent

devoir = must / have to

je	dois = I must / have to
tu	dois
il	doit
nous	devons
vous	devez
ils	doivent

dire = to say / tell

je	dis = I say / tell
tu	dis
il	dit
nous	disons
vous	dites
ils	disent

écrire = to write

j'	écris = I write
tu	écris
il	écrit
nous	écrivons
vous	écrivez
ils	écrivent

ALSO: | décrire | to describe |

faire = to do / make

je	fais = I do / make
tu	fais
il	fait
nous	faisons
vous	faites
ils	font

ALSO: | défaire | to undo |
| refaire | to redo |

lire = to read

je	lis = I read
tu	lis
il	lit
nous	lisons
vous	lisez
ils	lisent

mettre = to put

je	mets = I put (on)
tu	mets
il	met
nous	mettons
vous	mettez
ils	mettent

ALSO:
permettre	to allow / permit
promettre	to promise

ouvrir = to open

The present goes like a regular -**ER** verb.

j'	ouvre = I open
tu	ouvres
il	ouvre
nous	ouvrons
vous	ouvrez
ils	ouvrent

ALSO:
couvrir	to cover
découvrir	to discover

pouvoir = can / to be able

je	peux = I can / am able
tu	peux
il	peut
nous	pouvons
vous	pouvez
ils	peuvent

prendre = to take

je	prends = I take
tu	prends
il	prend
nous	prenons
vous	prenez
ils	prennent

ALSO:
apprendre	to learn
comprendre	to understand

recevoir = to receive / get

je	reçois = I receive
tu	reçois
il	reçoit
nous	recevons
vous	recevez
ils	reçoivent

savoir = to know

je	sais = I know (a fact)
tu	sais
il	sait
nous	savons
vous	savez
ils	savent

sortir = to go out

je	sors = I go out
tu	sors
il	sort
nous	sortons
vous	sortez
ils	sortent

ALSO:

mentir	to tell a lie
sentir	to feel
partir	to leave
dormir	to sleep
servir	to serve

venir = to come

je	viens = I come
tu	viens
il	vient
nous	venons
vous	venez
ils	viennent

ALSO:

devenir	to become
revenir	to come back
se souvenir de *	to remember
tenir	to hold
soutenir	to uphold

Reflexive. See page 25

voir = to see

je	vois = I see
tu	vois
il	voit
nous	voyons
vous	voyez
ils	voient

vouloir = to want

je	veux = I want
tu	veux
il	veut
nous	voulons
vous	voulez
ils	veulent

FOR MORE ADVANCED STUDENTS

suivre = to follow

je	suis = I follow
tu	suis
il	suit
nous	suivons
vous	suivez
ils	suivent

ALSO:

poursuivre	to pursue
see p.105	

craindre = to fear

je	crains = I fear
tu	crains
il	craint
nous	craignons
vous	craignez
ils	craignent

ALSO:

plaindre	to pity
se plaindre *	to complain
joindre	to join
rejoindre	to meet
éteindre	to switch off / put out

* Reflexive. See page 25

25
REFLEXIVE VERBS

In English you may have heard someone say, "sit yourself down." Quite a number of French verbs work like this. These are called **verbes pronominaux**.

se laver

je	me	lave
tu	te	laves
il	se	lave
nous	nous	lavons
vous	vous	lavez
ils	se	lavent

Note:
If you are washing a car, you say:
   Je lave la voiture

If you are washing yourself, you say:
   Je me lave

Here are some common Reflexive Verbs:

s'amuser	to enjoy yourself, to have fun (see page 109)
s'appeler	to be called (see page 14)
se brosser les dents	to brush your teeth
se coucher	to go to bed
se dépêcher	to hurry
s'endormir	to fall asleep (see page 23)
s'ennuyer	to be bored (see page 15)
s'entendre bien avec	to get on well with
s'habiller	to get dressed
s'installer	to settle (down)
se lever	to get up (see page 16)
se promener	to go for a walk (see page 16)
se rappeler	to remember (see page 14)
se raser	to shave
se reposer	to rest
se réveiller	to wake up

PERFECT – passé composé

This tense has 2 names:

1. **PARFAIT** = perfect, completely done
2. **PASSÉ COMPOSÉ** = past, composed of 2 words

You need an **AUXILIARY** (=helping) **VERB** + a **PAST PARTICIPLE**.

The **auxiliary verb** is nearly always **AVOIR**. So we say that most verbs are **conjugated** (=joined together) with **AVOIR**.

You can see how it works below.

The **past participle** of regular **-ER verbs** always ends in **–É**.

Eg: the past participle of **REGARDER** is *REGARDÉ*.

J'ai regardé: **I watched / I have watched / I did watch**

Here it is in full:

j'	ai	**regardé**
tu	as	**regardé**
il	a	**regardé**
nous	avons	**regardé**
vous	avez	**regardé**
ils	ont	**regardé**

The **past participle** of regular **-IR** verbs always ends in **–I**.

Eg: the past participle of **FINIR** is *FINI*.

j'	ai	fini = I finished / have finished
tu	as	fini
il	a	fini
nous	avons	fini
vous	avez	fini
ils	ont	fini

The **past participle** of regular **-RE** verbs always ends in **–U**.

Eg: the past participle of **VENDRE** is *VENDU*.

j'	ai	vendu = I sold / have sold
tu	as	vendu
il	a	vendu
nous	avons	vendu
vous	avez	vendu
ils	ont	vendu

The **past participles** of **IRREGULAR VERBS** fall into groups:

INFINITIVE	auxiliary	PAST PARTICIPLE	
prendre	j'ai	**pris**	I took
apprendre	j'ai	**appris**	I learnt
comprendre	j'ai	**compris**	I understood

mettre	j'ai	**mis**	I put
promettre	j'ai	**promis**	I promised
permettre	j'ai	**permis**	I allowed

-t The past participle in this group is identical with the "il" form of the Present Tense

dire	j'ai	**dit**	I said
faire	j'ai	**fait**	I made / did
écrire	j'ai	**écrit**	I wrote
conduire	j'ai	**conduit**	I drove

-i

dormir	j'ai	**dormi**	I slept
mentir	j'ai	**menti**	I lied
sentir	j'ai	**senti**	I felt
servir	j'ai	**servi**	I served
rire	j'ai	**ri**	I laughed
suivre	j'ai	**suivi**	I followed

être	j'ai	été	I was

-u			
avoir	j'ai	e**u**	I had
boire	j'ai	b**u**	I drank
croire	j'ai	cr**u**	I believed
devoir	j'ai	d**û**	I had to
lire	j'ai	l**u**	I read
pouvoir	j'ai	p**u**	I was able to
savoir	j'ai	s**u**	I knew
voir	j'ai	v**u**	I saw
battre	j'ai	batt**u**	I beat
connaître	j'ai	conn**u**	I knew (a person)
courir	j'ai	cour**u**	I ran
apercevoir	j'ai	aperç**u**	I noticed
recevoir	j'ai	reç**u**	I received / got
tenir	j'ai	ten**u**	I held
vouloir	j'ai	voul**u**	I wanted
il faut	il a	fall**u**	it was necessary
il pleut	il a	pl**u**	it rained

-t			
ouvr**ir**	j'ai	ouver**t**	I opened
couvr**ir**	j'ai	couver**t**	I covered
découvr**ir**	j'ai	découver**t**	I discovered

When the verb is conjugated with **AVOIR**, the **Past Participle** agrees with the **PRECEDING DIRECT OBJECT**.

> **NOTE:** In order to understand this, you need to know some grammatical terms.
>
> **Eg:** *The boy gave the book to his father*
> *The boy gave his father the book*
>
> **Subject:** *the boy*
> **Verb:** *gave*
> **Direct object:** *the book*
> **Indirect object:** *(to) his father*
>
> The **PRECEDING DIRECT OBJECT** (**PDO**)
> = the direct object which goes **before** the verb.

Eg:

La lettre? Oui, je l'ai lue. = The letter? Yes, I have read <u>it</u>.

Regardez les gâteaux que j'ai faits = Look at <u>the cakes which</u> I've made

Nous les lui avons montrés = We showed <u>them</u> to her

Il nous a regardés = He watched <u>us</u>

The vast majority of French Verbs are **conjugated** with **AVOIR**. There are, however, a number of important verbs conjugated with **ÊTRE** (the **auxiliary verb** is **ÊTRE**). *Eg:*

aller = to go

je	suis	**allé(e)**	I went
tu	es	**allé(e)**	you went
il	est	**allé**	he went
elle	est	**allée**	she went
nous	sommes	**allé(e)s**	we went
vous*	**êtes**	**allé(e)(s)**	you went*
ils	sont	**allés**	they went
elles	sont	**allées**	

When the Verb is conjugated with **ÊTRE**, the **past participle** agrees with the **SUBJECT**.

Eg: *La dame est arrivée* = The lady arrived
Nous sommes descendus = We went down
Les garçons sont rentrés = The boys went home
Elles sont venues = They came

***Vous** can be masculine/feminine singular or masculine/feminine plural. Adjust the past participle accordingly.
Eg: **allé / allée / allés / allées**

32

It is easy to remember which verbs are conjugated with **ÊTRE**. There are *5 pairs of opposites and some spares:*

arriver	je suis	arrivé	I arrived
partir	je suis	parti	I left

monter	je suis	monté	I went up
descendre	je suis	descendu	I went down

entrer	je suis	entré	I entered
sortir	je suis	sorti	I went out

venir	je suis	venu	I came
aller	je suis	allé	I went

naître	je suis	né	I was born
mourir	je suis	mort	I died

rentrer	je suis	rentré	I got home
rester	je suis	resté	I remained / stayed
retourner	je suis	retourné	I returned
tomber	je suis	tombé	I fell

33

All **REFLEXIVE verbs** are conjugated with **ÊTRE**.

The Past Participles of Reflexive Verbs <u>usually agree</u> with the SUBJECT.

Eg:

« **Je me suis couchée** », **dit Maman** = "I went to bed", says Mum

« **Je me suis amusée** », **dit Eloïse** = "I had a good time", says Eloïse

Elle s'est levée = She got up

Nous nous sommes habillés = We got dressed

Ils se sont rasés = They shaved

Elles se sont vues = They saw each other

Advanced students need to know:

Past Participles of Reflexive Verbs actually agree with – and only with – the **PDO** (if there is one). See page 30.

NB: the reflexive **se** in the following case is a **preceding INDIRECT Object**, because verbs such as téléphoner, parler, répondre, ordonner and dire are followed by <u>à quelqu'un</u> = to someone.

Eg: **Ils se sont téléphoné** = They phoned (to) each other

IMPERFECT – imparfait

This is very simple. Just take the stem from the **"nous"** form of the **present tense** and add

-ais
-ais
-ait
-ions
-iez
-aient

(je donnais: I was giving / I used to give)

	donnER	**finIR**	**vendRE**
je	donnais = I was giving	finissais = I was finishing	vendais = I used to sell
tu	donnais	finissais	vendais
il	donnait	finissait	vendait
nous	donnions	finissions	vendions
vous	donniez	finissiez	vendiez
ils	donnaient	finissaient	vendaient

Many students find it difficult to understand the difference in use between the **Passé Composé** and **Imparfait**. The **Passé Composé** is for ONE OFF events. **Imparfait** describes what was happening in the past, or how things were (background), or things that you did regularly, or you used to do.

Remember **g → ge** and **c → ç** before A, O, U: (see page 17)

	manger	**commencer**
je	mangeais = I was eating	commençais = I was beginning
tu	mangeais	commençais
il	mangeait	commençait
nous	mangions	commencions
vous	mangiez	commenciez
ils	mangeaient	commençaient

All other verbs follow the same pattern in the **IMPERFECT**, *ie*: the stem is the *nous* form of the present tense, minus the -**ons**.

Eg:

j'allais	I was going
j'avais	I used to have
je devais	I had to
j'écrivais	I was writing
je lisais	I was reading
je mettais	I was putting
j'ouvrais	I was opening
je pouvais	I was able
je prenais	I used to take
je venais	I used to come
je voulais	I wanted

The only truly **IRREGULAR** imperfect is **être**:

	être	
j'	étais	I was
tu	étais	you were
il	était	he was
nous	étions	we were
vous	étiez	you were
ils	étaient	they were

FUTURE – futur simple

The **future** is based on the INFINITIVE. Take the **infinitive**, chop off any final "-e", so that the stem of the FUTURE ends in 'r', and add the Present Tense of AVOIR:

-ai, -as, -a, -ons, -ez, -ont.

	donner	finir	attendre
je/j'	donnerai = I will give	finirai = I will finish	attendrai = I will wait
tu	donneras	finiras	attendras
il	donnera	finira	attendra
nous	donnerons	finirons	attendrons
vous	donnerez	finirez	attendrez
ils	donneront	finiront	attendront

Many verbs which are normally IRREGULAR are perfectly REGULAR in the FUTURE – see top of this page. *Eg:*

partir	je	partirai	I will leave
sortir	je	sortirai	I will go out
battre	je	battrai	I will beat
boire	je	boirai	I will drink
écrire	j'	écrirai	I will write
lire	je	lirai	I will read
mettre	je	mettrai	I will put
prendre	je	prendrai	I will take

There are some **IRREGULAR** future forms. Most of them are still based on the **INFINITIVE**, sometimes with one or two letters missing.

être	je	**ser**ai	I will be
avoir	j'	**aur**ai	I will have
savoir	je	**saur**ai	I will know
aller	j'	**ir**ai	I will go
faire	je	**fer**ai	I will do / make
devoir	je	**devr**ai	I will have to
envoyer	j'	**enverr**ai	I will send
voir	je	**verr**ai	I will see
pouvoir	je	**pourr**ai	I will be able to
courir	je	**courr**ai	I will run
tenir	je	**tiendr**ai	I will hold
venir	je	**viendr**ai	I will come
vouloir	je	**voudr**ai	I will want

ÊTRE (*je serai*) & **ALLER** (*j'irai*) have to be memorised.

NOTE: The changes (*see pp. 14-16*), which occur in some **-ER** verbs before a MUTE "**e**" in the Present, occur throughout the FUTURE, including the "**nous**" and "**vous**" forms:

appeler	j'	**appeller**ai	I will call
jeter	je	**jetter**ai	I will throw
essayer	j'	**essaier**ai	I will try
acheter	j'	**achèter**ai	I will buy

BUT "**espérer**", etc. use the infinitive as it stands with the "**é**" (**j'esp**é**rerai**).

CONDITIONAL – conditionnel

Take the **FUTURE stem** and add the **IMPERFECT endings**:
See pages 36-37   See page 34

	donner
je	donnerais = I would give
tu	donnerais
il	donnerait
nous	donnerions
vous	donneriez
ils	donneraient

ALL VERBS follow this pattern in the CONDITIONAL tense.

je	finirais	I would finish
je	vendrais	I would sell
je	partirais	I would leave
je	boirais	I would drink
je	mettrais	I would put
je	prendrais	I would take
je	serais	I would be
j'	aurais	I would have
j'	irais	I would go
je	ferais	I would do
je	devrais	I ought to
je	pourrais	I could / might
je	verrais	I would see
je	viendrais	I would come

These verbs appear in the same order as those in the Future Tense on pages 36-37

PLUPERFECT – plus-que-parfait

The PLUPERFECT is exactly like the PERFECT, but the **auxiliary verb** is in the IMPERFECT. *See pages 26-33*

		donner
j'	avais	donné = I had given
tu	avais	donné
il	avait	donné
nous	avions	donné
vous	aviez	donné
ils	avaient	donné

		venir
j'	étais	venu = I had come
tu	étais	venu
il	était	venu
nous	étions	venus
vous	étiez	venus
ils	étaient	venus

The following page contains examples of sentences using the Pluperfect.

Example sentences using the Pluperfect

J'ai vu ^{I saw} que ^{that} le train **était parti** ^{had left}

J'ai entendu dire ^{heard it said} que le directeur ^{headteacher} **avait pris** ^{had taken} sa retraite ^{his retirement}

J'ai compris ^{I understood} qu'on ^{that someone} **avait volé** ^{had stolen} mon vélo ^{my bicycle}

Je me suis aperçu ^{I perceived} qu'il ^{that he} **avait menti** ^{had been lying}

J'ai dit ^{I said} que ^{that} j'**avais reçu** ^{I had received} un prix ^{a prize}

J'ai confirmé ^{I confirmed} que ^{that} j'**avais réservé** ^{I had reserved} 4 places ^{4 seats}

J'ai expliqué ^{I explained} qu'il y **avait eu** ^{that there had been} un accident ^{an accident}

J'ai été ^{I was} fâché ^{cross} parce que ^{because} j'**avais voulu** ^{I had wanted} voir ^{to watch} ce film ^{that film}

J'ai été ^{I was} surpris ^{surprised} parce que ^{because} je n'**avais** pas **entendu** ^{I had not heard} le bruit ^{the noise}

J'**étais allé** ^{I had gone (had walked)} au cinéma ^{to the cinema} à pied ^{on foot}

Mon père ^{My father} était fâché ^{was cross} parce que ^{because} j'**étais rentré** ^{I had come home} si tard ^{so late}

Ma mère ^{My mother} était ravie/enchantée ^{was delighted} parce que j'**avais réussi** ^{I had passed} à mes examens ^{my exams}

PAST HISTORIC – passé simple

The Narrative in most books, including children's books, is written in the **past historic**. You will never hear it in conversation, but you need to be able to recognise it.

It is very easy to recognise which verb is being used:

je donnai = I gave

The PAST HISTORIC has 3 types of endings.

1. -ai, -as, -a, -âmes, -âtes, -èrent → used for regular -**ER** verbs, + **aller**

	donner	**aller**
je / j'	donnai	allai
tu	donnas	allas
il	donna	alla
nous	donnâmes	allâmes
vous	donnâtes	allâtes
ils	donnèrent	allèrent

2. -**is**, -**is**, -**it**, -**îmes**, -**îtes**, -**irent** → used for regular -**IR** and -**RE** verbs, + irregular verbs listed below

	finir	**descendre**
je	finis	descendis
tu	finis	descendis
il	finit	descendit
nous	finîmes	descendîmes
vous	finîtes	descendîtes
ils	finirent	descendirent

IRREGULAR verbs:

s'asseoir *to sit*	je	m'assis
conduire	je	conduisis
craindre *to fear*	je	craignis
dire	je	dis
dormir	je	dormis
écrire	j'	écrivis
faire	je	fis

mettre	je	mis
ouvrir	j'	ouvris
partir	je	partis
prendre	je	pris
sortir	je	sortis
suivre *to follow*	je	suivis
voir	je	vis

3. -us, -us, -ut, -ûmes, -ûtes, -urent → used for irregular verbs listed below

être	je	fus
avoir	j'	eus

boire	je	bus
courir	je	courus
devoir	je	dus

il faut	il	fallut
lire	je	lus
pouvoir	je	pus
recevoir	je	reçus
savoir	je	sus
vouloir	je	voulus

Venir, tenir *(and their compounds)*, etc. are IRREGULAR:

je	vins
tu	vins
il	vint
nous	vînmes
vous	vîntes
ils	vinrent

je	tins
tu	tins
il	tint
nous	tînmes
vous	tîntes
ils	tinrent

Example sentences using the Past Historic

Le roi Harold *King Harold* **arriva** *arrived* en France *in France*

Le prisonnier *The prisoner* **saisit** *seized* le bâton *the stick*

Les soldats *The soldiers* **prirent** *took* les bateaux *the boats*

Je **voyageai** *I travelled* en Suisse *in Switzerland*

When to use which tense

L'INDICATIF PRÉSENT = PRESENT

What you are doing now, or what you usually do.

normalement	normally
d'habitude	usually
aujourd'hui	today

je travaille = I work / am working / do work

PASSÉ COMPOSÉ = PERFECT

Actions in the past which are complete/ finished.

hier	yesterday
la semaine dernière	last week

j'ai travaillé = I worked / have worked / did work

IMPARFAIT = IMPERFECT

Describing what was happening in the past, or how things were (background), or things that you did regularly, or you used to do. **Based on NOUS form of Present.**

quand j'avais 15 ans	when I was 15

je travaillais = I used to work / was working

45

LE FUTUR SIMPLE = FUTURE

Things that will happen. **Based on INFINITIVE**

demain	tomorrow
la semaine prochaine	next week

je travaillerai = I will work

LE CONDITIONNEL = CONDITIONAL

Things that would / might happen if…

si j'étais riche…	if I were rich…

je travaillerais = I would work

LE PLUS-QUE-PARFAIT = PLUPERFECT

What had already happened before the time you are talking about.

j'avais oublié mes clefs	I had forgotten my keys

j'avais travaillé = I had worked

LE PASSÉ SIMPLE = PAST HISTORIC

It is useful to recognise this tense because it is the narrative tense in all books.

j'allai à Paris	I went to Paris

je travaillai = I worked

EXAMPLES

PRESENT:

- *Il **fait** beau aujourd'hui.* It's fine today.
- *D'habitude le jeudi je **joue** au tennis.*
  Usually I play tennis on Thursdays.
- *Ma sœur **prépare** le déjeuner.* My sister is preparing lunch.
- *Tous les soirs mon père **lit** le journal.*
  Every evening my father reads the newspaper.

PERFECT:

- *Récemment j'**ai vu** un film.* Recently I saw a film.
- *Hier ma tante **a acheté** une jupe.*
  Yesterday my aunt bought a skirt.
- *Le weekend passé, nous **sommes allés** à Paris.*
  Last weekend we went to Paris.
- *Ce matin, je me **suis levé**(e), à six heures.*
  This morning I got up at 6 a.m.

IMPERFECT:

- *Quand j'**étais** petite, je **jouais** avec mes poupées.*
  When I was little I used to play with my dolls.
- *Le soleil **brillait**, les oiseaux **chantaient**.*
  The sun was shining, the birds were singing.
- *Elle **lisait** un roman quand son frère est arrivé.*
  She was reading a novel when her brother arrived.

FUTURE:

- *Lundi prochain, j'**irai** en France.*
    Next Monday I <u>shall go</u> to France.
- *Demain maman **fera** ses courses.*
    Tomorrow Mum <u>will do</u> her shopping.
- *Après-demain ils **partiront** en vacances.*
    The day after tomorrow they <u>will go</u> on holiday.

CONDITIONAL:

- *Si j'étais riche, je **voyagerais** dans le monde entier.*
    If I were rich, I <u>would travel</u> round the whole world.
- *S'il avait une voiture, il **irait** en Ecosse.*
    If he had a car, he <u>would go</u> to Scotland.
- *S'ils voulaient partir, ils **pourraient** aller loin.*
    If they wanted to leave, they <u>could</u> go far.
- ***Pourrais**-tu me passer le sel, s'il te plaît.*
    <u>Could</u> you pass me the salt, please.

PLUPERFECT: (see also page 40)

- *Je me suis rendu compte que j'**avais perdu** mon passeport.* I realised that I <u>had lost</u> my passport.
- *J'ai découvert que j'**avais oublié** ma brosse à dents.*
    I discovered that I <u>had forgotten</u> my toothbrush.

PAST HISTORIC: (see also page 43)

- *Il **alla** en Autriche.* He <u>went</u> to Austria.

48
Le Négatif

ne	verbe	pas	not
ne		plus	no more / no longer / none left
ne		rien	nothing / not anything
ne		jamais	never
ne		personne	nobody
ne		nulle part	nowhere / not anywhere
ne		ni… ni	neither… nor
ne		que	only

Eg:

je <u>ne</u> vois <u>pas</u> _{can't see} le cahier _{exercise book}

je <u>n'</u>écoute _{am not listening} <u>rien</u> _{to anything}

il <u>ne</u> sourit <u>jamais</u> _{never smiles}

vous <u>n'</u>avez <u>plus</u> _{have no more} de farine _{flour}

ils <u>ne</u> courent <u>plus</u> _{aren't running any more}

ils <u>n'</u>écrivent _{write} à <u>personne</u> _{nobody}

elles <u>ne</u> vont _{are not going} <u>nulle part</u> _{anywhere}

nous n'avons [have] ni [neither] jambon [ham] ni [nor] veau [veal]

vous n'avez [have] qu'une [only one] armoire [wardrobe]

You can use 2 or 3 negatives together

il ne vient plus jamais [never comes any more] chez nous [to our house]

il ne doit plus [no longer owes] rien [anything]

Rien + personne can be the subject of the verb.

rien [nothing] ne l'intéresse [interests him/her]

personne [nobody] ne dort [is sleeping] ici [here]

2 verbs in a negative sentence

If there are two verbs *together* in a negative sentence, it is usually the first one that is negative. *Eg:*

je ne vais pas [I am not going] sortir [to go out]

il ne veut pas [he does not want] travailler [to work]

elle ne peut pas [she can't] aller [go] au cinéma [to the cinema]

ils ne savent pas [they can't] nager [swim]

The Negative with other tenses

on ne mangeait jamais *we never ate* de poisson *fish*

il ne commençait son travail qu'à minuit *he only started his work at midnight*

je ne la verrai plus jamais *I will never ever see her again*

l'auteur *the author* n'écrira *will write* plus rien *nothing more*

tu ne répondras *you won't reply* à personne *to anyone*

il ne reconnaîtrait *he wouldn't recognize* personne *anyone*

nous n'irions *we wouldn't be going* nulle part *anywhere*

The Negative in Compound Tenses – Passé Composé, Plus-que-Parfait, etc.

je n'ai pas entendu *I didn't hear* la sonnerie *the bell ring*

je ne lui ai pas écrit *I didn't write to him/her*

elle ne lui a pas offert *she didn't give him/her* de cadeau *a present*

il ne m'a pas expliqué le problème *he didn't explain the problem to me*

Note the "ne" comes immediately **after** the **Subject**.

The "pas" comes **before** the **Past Participle**.

51
Questions

Poser ^{to ask/put/pose} une question

There are 3 ways of asking Questions in French.

<u>You often raise your voice on the last syllable.</u>

1. Simply make a statement but raise your voice on the last syllable. (See arrows)
2. Place *Est-ce que* before the statement.
3. Invert Subject + Verb.

Il est beau?	
*Est-ce qu'*il est beau?	Is he good-looking?
Est-il beau?	

Pierre est intelligent?	
Est-ce que Pierre est intelligent?	Is Pierre intelligent?
Pierre est-il intelligent?	

Elle est jolie?	
*Est-ce qu'*elle est jolie?	Is she pretty?
Est-elle jolie?	

Lucie est douée?	
Est-ce que Lucie est douée?	Is Lucy gifted?
Lucie est-elle douée?	

Les enfants ne sont pas sages?	Aren't the children good /well-behaved?
Est-ce que les enfants ne sont pas sages?	
Les enfants ne sont-ils pas sages?	

In these 2 examples you add -t before -il/-elle (because the verb ends in a vowel)

Il a un ballon?	Does he have a ball?
Est-ce qu'il a un ballon?	
A-t-il un ballon?	

Elle regarde le film?	Is she watching the film?
Est-ce qu'elle regarde le film?	
Regarde-t-elle le film?	

Inversion using "je" (<u>Only these 4 Verbs</u> can be inverted in the "je" form.)

Each of these is spoken as a single syllable:

être	suis-je?	am I?
aller	vais-je?	am I going?
avoir	ai-je?	have I?
pouvoir	(je peux becomes) puis-je?	may I?

Questions in Perfect Tense

Tu as fait un gâteau?
Est-ce que tu as fait un gâteau?
As-tu fait un gâteau?

Did/have you made a cake?

Où êtes-vous ^{Did you} allé(e) ? ^{go}

Où avez-vous ^{Did you} passé ^{spend} les^{the} vacances? ^{holidays}

Qu'est-ce que ^{What} vous avez ^{did you} fait ^{do} à Paris?

Il a fait ^{Was it (the weather)} beau ^{fine}?

See also Useful Questions on page 58.

Plus Grammar Tips

This section is intended to clarify a few common misunderstandings. It is not a comprehensive outline of French grammar. Your text book should provide that. These pages have proved useful to numerous students.

Colour codes (used where useful)

Masculine – blue
Feminine – red
Plural – green
English - purple

55

Le La Les = the

Masc. singular	Fem. singular	Masc+Fem before vowel/h	Plural	English
le	la	l'	les	the
un	une		des	a
au	à la	à l'	aux	to/at the
du	de la	de l'	des	of/from the
mon	ma	mon ami(e)	mes	my
ton	ta	ton ami(e)	tes	your
son	sa	son ami(e)	ses	his/her
notre	notre		nos	our
votre	votre		vos	your
leur	leur		leurs	their
ce	cette	cet	ces	this/that
quel	quelle		quels quelles	which
lequel	laquelle		lesquels lesquelles	which one
auquel	à laquelle		auxquels auxquelles	to/at which
duquel	de laquelle		desquels desquelles	of/from which
celui	celle		ceux/celles	the one(s)
chacun	chacune			each one

If the person or thing you are talking about is <u>masculine singular</u>, use the BLUE column.

If the person or thing you are talking about is <u>feminine singular</u>, use the RED column.

If the persons or things you are talking about are <u>plural</u>, use the GREEN column.

Examples :

père is masculine singular.

So :

le père	the father
un père	a father
au père	to the father
du père	the father's / of the father
mon père	my father
ton père	your father
son père	his/her father
notre père	our father
votre père	your father
leur père	their father
ce père	this father
quel père	which father

mère is feminine singular.

la mère	the mother
une mère	a mother
à la mère	to the mother
de la mère	the mother's / of the mother
ma mère	my mother
ta mère	your mother
sa mère	his/her mother
notre mère	our mother
votre mère	your mother
leur mère	their mother
cette mère	this mother
quelle mère	which mother

parents is plural.

les parents	the parents
des parents	parents
aux parents	to the parents
des parents	the parents' / of the parents
mes parents	my parents
tes parents	your parents
ses parents	his/her parents
nos parents	our parents
vos parents	your parents
leurs parents	their parents
ces parents	these parents
quels parents	which parents

58
Useful questions

(see also pp.51-53)

Qu'est-ce que c'est? What is it?

Comment vous appelez-vous? What's your name? (to an adult)

Comment t'appelles-tu? What's your name?

Comment *How* ça s'écrit? do you spell that?

Où *Where* habitez-vous? do you live? (to an adult)

Où *Where* habites-tu? do you live?

C'est où ça? Where's that?   Ça se trouve où? Where is that?

Connais-tu *Do you know* Londres *London*? (*Londres* is essentially a single syllable)

Qu'en penses-tu? What do you think of it?

Tu t'intéresses *Are you interested* à la lecture *in reading*?

La musique de Chopin te plaît? Do you like Chopin's music?

Où vas-tu *Where are you going* passer *to spend* les grandes vacances *the summer holidays*? Comment *How* voyageras-tu? will you travel?

Tu es *Are you* sportif *sporty*?

Quels sports *Which sports* préfères-tu *do you like best*?

Tu as vu *Have you seen* ce film *that film*?

De quoi s'agit-il? What's it about?

Pour aller à la banque, *The way to the bank* s'il vous plaît ? please?

Qu'est-ce que vous avez comme crêpes ? What sort of pancakes do you have?

59
Opinions

Quel est votre avis ? What is your opinion ?

à mon avis — in my opinion
selon moi — according to me
je pense que — I think that
je crois que — I believe that
je trouve que — I find that
je trouve cela intelligent — I find that clever
je suis sûr(e) que — I am sure that
j'estime que — I think that
j'imagine que — I imagine that
je suppose que — I suppose that
je dirais que — I would say that
il me semble que — it seems to me that
bien sûr — of course
naturellement — naturally
décidément — definitely
certainement — certainly
sans doute — doubtless / without doubt
j'en suis sûr — I am sure of it

c'est	it is
ce sont	they are
ce n'est pas	it isn't
est-ce ?	is it?
n'est-ce pas ?	isn't it?
ça a été	it was (one off)
c'était	it was
ce sera	it will be
ce serait	it would be

You can **express your opinions** with phrases from the left. The **ADJECTIVES** pp.69-77 may provide some ideas. You can **justify your opinion** with **forms of c'est**, also using Adjectives. *Eg*:

Je trouve que (I think) les jeunes (young people) aimeront (will like) ce film (this film) parce que (because) c'est (it is) marrant (funny)

Je dirais (would say) que l'excursion était décevante (disappointing) parce que ça a été mal (badly) organisée (organised)

Agreement

je suis du ^{of the} même ^{same} avis ^{opinion}

je suis d'accord ^{I agree}

c'est ^{that is} tout à fait ^{absolutely} mon ^{my} avis ^{opinion}

Uncertainty

il y a ^{there are} du pour ^{(arguments) for} et du contre ^{against}

je ne sais pas ^{I don't know}

ça ^{that} dépend ^{depends}

je ne suis pas ^{I am not} entièrement ^{entirely} d'accord ^{in agreement}

Disagreement

ce n'est pas ^{that is not} (du tout ^{at all}) mon ^{my} avis ^{opinion}

je ne suis pas ^{I am not} (du tout ^{at all}) d'accord ^{in agreement}

Qualifying remarks

ça, c'est ^{that is} très important ^{very important}

pour moi, ^{in my view,}

ça n'a pas ^{that isn't} beaucoup d'importance ^{very important}

61

Stressed pronouns

Also called strong or emphatic pronouns

Subject	Stressed pronoun	
je	moi	I/me
tu	toi	you
il	lui	he/him
elle	elle	she/her
on	soi	one
nous	nous	we/us
vous	vous	you
ils	eux	(m) they/them
elles	elles	(f) they/them

How to use: it's me, myself, I, and to me

A – it's me

c'est moi	it's I/me
c'est toi	it's you
c'est lui	it's he/him
c'est elle	it's she/her
c'est nous	it's we/us
c'est vous	it's you
ce sont eux	it's they/them
ce sont elles	it's they/them

B – myself

moi-même		myself
toi-même	etc.	yourself
nous-mêmes	etc.	ourselves

C – for stress

| Moi, je travaille | **I**'m working |
| toi, tu regardes la télé | **You**'re watching TV |

D – with prepositions

à moi	to me
avant elle	before her
avec nous	with us
chez moi	at my house / at home
dans eux	in them
de lui	of him
derrière soi	behind one
devant nous	in front of us
en vous	in you
entre nous	between us
envers nous	(feeling) towards us
parmi eux	amongst them
pour lui	for him
sans vous	without you
sous elles	under them (f)
sur moi	on me
vers elles	towards them (f)

63

à = to/at

English	Masc. singular	Fem. singular	Masc+Fem before vowel/h	Plural
to/at the	~~à + le~~ **au**	à + la	à + l'	~~à + les~~ **aux**
		à + la	**à + l'**	

Masculine singular - **au** = to/at the	au	bar	to/at the	bar
	au	bowling	to/at the	bowling alley
	au	café	to/at the	café
	au	camping	to/at the	campsite
	au	centre commercial	to/at the	shopping centre
	au	centre sportif	to/at the	sports centre
	au	château	to/at the	castle
	au	collège	to/at the	secondary school
	au	commissariat de police	to/at the	police station
	au	marché	to/at the	market
	au	musée	to/at the	museum
	au	parc	to/at the	park
	au	parking	to/at the	car park
	au	pont	to/at the	bridge
	au	poste de pompiers	to/at the	fire station
	au	restaurant	to/at the	restaurant
	au	rez-de-chaussée	on the	ground floor
	au	stade	to/at the	stadium
	au	supermarché	to/at the	supermarket
	au	syndicat d'initiative	to/at the	tourist office
	au	terrain de foot	to/at the	football field
	au	terrain de jeux	to/at the	playground
	au	théâtre	to/at the	theatre

Feminine singular - **à la** = to/at the	à la	banque	to/at the	bank
	à la	bibliothèque	to/at the	library
	à la	boucherie	to/at the	butcher's
	à la	boulangerie	to/at the	baker's
	à la	boutique	to/at the	shop
	à la	cathédrale	to/at the	cathedral
	à la	charcuterie	to/at the	pork butcher's
	à la	forêt	to/at the	forest
	à la	librairie	to/at the	book shop
	à la	mairie	to/at the	town hall
	à la	patinoire	to/at the	skating rink
	à la	pharmacie	to/at the	pharmacy
	à la	piscine	to/at the	swimming pool
	à la	plage	to/at the	beach
	à la	poste	to/at the	post office
	à la	rivière	to/at the	river

Masculine/Feminine singular beginning with a vowel/h – **à l'** = to/at the	à l'	arrêt de bus	to/at the	bus stop
	à l'	auberge de jeunesse	to/at the	youth hostel
	à l'	école (primaire)	to/at the	(primary) school
	à l'	église	to/at the	church
	à l'	épicerie	to/at the	grocer's
	à l'	étranger		abroad
	à l'	hôpital	to/at the	hospital
	à l'	hôtel	to/at the	hotel
	à l'	hôtel de ville	to/at the	town hall
	à l'	office de tourisme	to/at the	tourist office
	à l'	université	to/at the	university

Plural - **aux** = to/at the	aux	bureaux	to/at the	offices
	aux	Etats-Unis	to/at the	USA
	aux	magasins	to/at the	shops

65

de = of/from

English	Masc. singular	Fem. singular	Masc+Fem before vowel/h	Plural
of/from the	~~de + le~~ **du**	de + la **de la**	de + l' **de l'**	~~de + les~~ **des**

Masculine singular – **du** = of/from the	du	caissier	of the cashier/the cashier's
	du	Canada	from Canada
	du	coiffeur	of the hairdresser/the hairdresser's
	du	dactylo	of the typist/the typist's
	du	garçon	of the boy/the boy's
	du	Japon	from Japan
	du	médecin	of the doctor/the doctor's
	du	père	of the father/the father's
	du	quai	from the platform
	du	serveur	of the waiter/the waiter's
	du	vendeur	of the sales assistant/the sales assistant's

Feminine singular – **de la** = of/from the	de la	coiffeuse	of the hairdresser/the hairdresser's
	de la	cuisinière	of the cook/the cook's
	de la	gare	from the station
	de la	Grèce	from Greece
	de la	Manche	from the English Channel
	de la	mère	of the mother/the mother's
	de la	Seine	from the Seine
	de la	sœur	of the sister/the sister's
	de la	Suisse	from Switzerland
	de la	tante	of the aunt/the aunt's

Masc or Fem singular beginning with a vowel/h – **de l'** = of/from the	de l'	agent	of the policeman/the policeman's
	de l'	ami(e)	of the friend/the friend's
	de l'	Asie	from Asia
	de l'	avocat	of the lawyer/the lawyer's
	de l'	employé(e)	of the clerk/the clerk's of the employee/the employee's
	de l'	Europe	from Europe
	de l'	Inde	from India
	de l'	Italie	from Italy

Plural – **des** = of/from the	des	Alpes	from the Alps
	des	enfants	of the children/the children's
	des	Etats-Unis	from USA
	des	malades	of the patients/the patients'
	des	parents	of the parents/the parents'
	des	Pays-Bas	from Holland
	des	voleurs	of the thieves/the thieves'

du/de la/des also mean 'some'

Masculine singular	du	café	some	coffee
	du	cidre	some	cider
	du	fromage	some	cheese
	du	lait	some	milk
	du	potage	some	soup
	du	poulet	some	chicken
	du	sucre	some	sugar
	du	thé	some	tea
Feminine singular	de la	bière	some	beer
	de la	brume	some	mist
	de la	charcuterie	some	selection of cold meats/delicatessen
	de la	lecture	some	reading
	de la	limonade	some	lemonade
	de la	monnaie	some	change
	de la	musique	some	music
	de la	neige	some	snow
Masc./Fem. singular beginning with a vowel/h	de l'	agneau	some	lamb
	de l'	ail	some	garlic
	de l'	argent	some	money
	de l'	eau minérale	some	mineral water
Plural	des	haricots	some	beans
	des	petits pois	some	peas
	des	pommes de terre	some	potatoes
	des	cartes	some	cards
	des	problèmes	some	problems
	des	pièces (de monnaie)	some	coins

68
du, de la, des >> de / d'

1. After a Negative

je n'ai plus *I've got no more* d'encre *ink*

il ne reste plus *Lit: there remains no more* de papier *paper* (= there's no paper left)

il n'y a pas *there aren't any* de feutres *felt-tips*

il n'achètera pas *he will not buy* de cigarettes *any cigarettes*

nous ne gagnerons jamais *we will never earn* d'argent *any money*

2. After Expressions of Quantity

beaucoup *lots* d'élèves *of pupils*

peu *few* de gens *people*

un kilo *a kilo* de pommes *of apples*

un demi-kilo *½ kilo* d'abricots (m) *of apricots*

100 grammes *100 grams* de beurre (m) *of butter*

un paquet *a packet* de biscuits (m) *of biscuits*

une boîte *a tin* de viande (f) *of meat*

un verre *a glass* de vin (m) *of wine*

une tasse *a cup* de café (m) *of coffee*

3. When Adjective precedes Noun

de bonnes *nice* gens *people*

de belles *beautiful* photos (f)

de vieilles *old* dames (f) *ladies*

69
Les Adjectifs

In the DICTIONARY, ADJECTIVES are usually printed :

grand, e = grand (m.s), grande (f.s) = big, tall

Plural. Add 's' to Singular.

This is the normal pattern :

	Singular	Plural
masculine	petit *	petits little, small, short
feminine	petite	petites

petit, e = little, small, short

You will notice that the feminine form often sounds very different from the masculine form.

As the French have heard these differences since babyhood, your spoken French will sound much more natural if you use the correct forms. Listen to the video to hear the difference.

NB: Most French Adjectives go AFTER the Noun.
***The highlighted Adjectives go BEFORE the Noun**

70

Some useful Regular Adjectives like "petit"

amusant	funny	intelligent	intelligent
assaisonné	highly seasoned	intéressant	interesting
barbant	boring	joli *	pretty
bavard	chatty	laid	ugly
bleu	blue	lourd	heavy
bruyant	noisy	maladroit	clumsy
charmant	charming	malsain	unhealthy
content	happy	mauvais *	bad
décevant	disappointing	marrant	funny
décontracté	relaxed	méchant	naughty
dégoûtant	disgusting	meilleur *	better (best)
distrait	absent-minded	motivé	motivated
doué	gifted	obstiné	obstinate
élégant	elegant	parfait	perfect
embêtant	annoying	passionnant	exciting
excellent	excellent	patient	patient
fatigant	tiring	piquant	spicy
fatigué	tired	poli	polite
fort	strong	préféré	favourite
grand *	big/tall	sain	healthy
idiot	idiotic	satisfaisant	satisfying
impatient	impatient	sûr de soi	self-confident
impoli	impolite	surdoué	highly gifted

The easiest Adjectives are those ending in silent 'e'

	Singular	Plural
masculine & feminine	riche	riches rich

As there is already an 'e' in the masculine form, you don't need to add an 'e' to the feminine form. This 'e' is silent.

Similar

agréable	pleasant
autre *	other
bête	stupid
célèbre	famous
chaque *	each
commode	convenient
difficile	difficult
effroyable	appalling
égoïste	selfish
épouvantable	dreadful
extraordinaire	extraordinary
facile	easy

formidable	great
inutile	useless
jaune	yellow
jeune *	young
libre	free, vacant
magnifique	magnificent
malade	ill
moderne	modern
pauvre	poor
propre	clean
rapide	fast
remarquable	remarkable
ridicule	ridiculous
rouge	red
sage	well-behaved
sale	dirty
sensible	sensitive
sévère	strict
sociable	sociable
splendide	splendid
sympathique	nice
terrible	wicked
triste	sad
utile	useful
vide	empty

There are quite a lot of

IRREGULAR ADJECTIVES

Once you know the **masculine** and **feminine** **singular**, you can work out the rest.

If the masculine singular ends in '**s**' or '**x**', you don't need to add an 's' for masculine plural.

	Singular	Plural
masculine	heureux	heureux happy
feminine	heureuse	heureuses

Similar

affreux	dreadful
courageux	brave
creux	hollow
curieux	curious
délicieux	delicious
désastreux	disastrous
ennuyeux	boring
furieux	furious

généreux	generous
malheureux	unhappy
mystérieux	mysterious
nombreux	numerous
paresseux	lazy
sérieux	serious
silencieux	silent

74

	Singular	Plural
masculine	gris	gris ^grey
feminine	grise	grises

Similar:	assis	seated, sitting
	* mauvais	bad

masc.	national	nationaux ^national
fem.	nationale	nationales

Similar:	expérimental	experimental
	illégal	illegal
	international	international
	légal	legal
	régional	regional
	spécial	special

masc.	naturel	naturels ^natural
fem.	naturelle	naturelles

Similar:	cruel	cruel
	officiel	official
	* quel	which
	gentil	nice/kind

75

masc.	premier *	premiers first
fem.	première	premières

Similar:
* cher	dear, expensive
dernier	last
entier	whole
familier	familiar

masc.	gros *	gros big, fat
fem.	grosse	grosses

Similar:
épais	thick

masc.	moyen	moyens average
fem.	moyenne	moyennes

Similar:
indien	Indian
canadien	Canadian

masc.	jaloux	jaloux jealous
fem.	jalouse	jalouses
masc.	doux	doux soft, gentle, sweet
fem.	douce	douces
masc.	fou	fous mad
fem.	folle	folles

76

	Singular	Plural
masc.	bon *	bons good
fem.	bonne	bonnes
masc.	blanc	blancs white
fem.	blanche	blanches
masc.	long *	longs long
fem.	longue	longues
masc.	frais	frais fresh/cool
fem.	fraîche	fraîches
masc.	travailleur	travailleurs hard-working
fem.	travailleuse	travailleuses
masc.	sportif	sportifs sporty
fem.	sportive	sportives

Similar:
actif	active
agressif	aggressive

masc.	public	publics public
fem.	publique	publiques
masc.	complet	complets complete
fem.	complète	complètes

Similar: inquiet worried

masc.	sec *	secs dry
fem.	sèche	sèches
masc.	tout *	tous all
fem.	toute	toutes
masc.	beau * bel before vowel/h	beaux beautiful, handsome
fem.	belle	belles

Similar: nouveau * new

masc.	vieux vieil before vowel/h	vieux old
fem.	vieille	vieilles

Most French Adjectives go AFTER the Noun.

These highlighted Adjectives go BEFORE the Noun

A few Adjectives change their meaning depending on whether they go BEFORE or AFTER the Noun. *Eg:*

ma propre chemise	my own shirt
ma chemise propre	my clean shirt
la dernière semaine	the last week (of term, etc.)
la semaine dernière	last week (the one that's just passed)
un ancien élève	a former pupil
une église ancienne	an ancient church

78
Object Pronouns

Me, him, to me, to her, them, etc. seem tricky in French. That is only because the word order sounds so odd to an English ear. You're saying things like:

- 'He to me it gives'
- 'They them there put'
- 'You of them have'

Once you learn the table below which sets out the <u>order</u> to put them in and you remember to put them **before** the <u>Verb</u>, you'll soon master them. D.I. = Direct Object   I.O. = Indirect Object

D.I. & I.O.	D.I.	I.O.		
me me / to me **te** you / to you **se** (to) himself / (to) herself/itself/oneself **nous** us / to us **vous** you / to you	**le** him/it (m) **la** her/it (f) **les** them	**lui** to him (m) / to her (f) **leur** to them	**y** to it / at it / on it / there	**en** of it / of them / some

THE RULE — These <u>Object Pronouns</u> go in the **above order** **BEFORE** the **VERB** EXCEPT IN A POSITIVE COMMAND

English and French verbs sometimes differ as to whether they take a Direct or Indirect Object. Don't worry too much about that. For the differences between a **Direct Object** and an **Indirect Object**, see page 30.

All these examples follow the order of the columns on page 78.

tu	**me**	regardes	you are watching	me
il	**me**	parle	he is speaking	to me
il	**te**	téléphone	he is telephoning	you
je	**t'**	attends	I am waiting	for you
elle	**se**	lave	she is washing	(herself)
il	**nous**	voit	he sees	us
elles	**nous**	parlent	they are talking	to us
je	**vous**	entends	I hear	you
ils	**vous**	disent bonjour	they say hello	to you
elle	**le**	quitte	she leaves	him
je	**le**	fais	I do	it (m)
tu	**la**	reçois	you receive	her/it (f)
il	**les**	ouvre	he opens	them
nous	**lui**	expliquons	we explain	to him
ils	**leur**	demandent	they ask	(to) them
elle	**y**	va	she goes	there
vous	**y**	mettez le livre	you put the book	on it
elles	**y**	descendent	they go down	there
tu	**en**	manges	you eat	some
elle	**en**	veut	she wants	some
il y	**en**	a	there is/are	some
j'	**en**	ai dix	I have ten	(of them)
nous	**en**	achetons un kilo	we buy a kilo	(of them)

Using 2 object pronouns together

The pronouns go in the order shown in the table on p.78 before the verb.

je	te	le	donne	I give	it (m)	to you
il	me	les	envoie	he is sending	them	to me
tu	nous	la	montres	you show	it (f)	to us
nous	vous	l'	apportons	we are bringing	it (f)	to you
je	le	lui	emprunte	I am borrowing	it (m)	from him
tu	la	lui	prêtes	you are lending	it (f)	to her
elle	le	leur	laisse	she is leaving	it (m)	for them
nous	les	leur	racontons	we are relating	them	to them
vous	l'	y	vendez	you sell	it	there
ils	les	y	mettent	they are putting	them	there
tu	m'	en	achètes	you are buying	some	for me
il	t'	en	écrit	he is writing	you (some)	some (for you)
nous	vous	y en	faisons	we are making	some there	for you
ils	y	en	font	they are making	some	there

Pronouns and Negatives

je ne	les	aime pas	I don't like	them	
tu ne	la	verras plus	you won't see	her	any more
je n'	y	vais jamais	I never go	there	
ils ne	m'	offrent rien	they offer	me	nothing

Pronouns with the Perfect Tense

je	l'	ai mangé	I have eaten	it	
il	t'	a vu	he saw	you	
nous	les	avons entendus *	we heard	them	
vous	la lui	avez donnée *	you gave	it (f)	to him
ils	les leur	ont envoyés *	they sent	them	to them
j'	y	suis allé	I went	there	
nous	y en	avons trouvé	we found	some	there

* see page 30 for Agreement of Past Participle with avoir

Pronouns & Negatives with the Perfect Tense

je n'	y	suis pas retourné	I didn't return there
tu ne	les	as pas cherchés	you didn't look for them
elle ne	vous	a pas entendu	she didn't hear you

Notice that ne comes immediately after the Subject and pas comes immediately before the Past Participle.

Positive Commands are different

Donne-**le**-moi !	Give it to me!
Ecoute-**la** !	Listen to her!
Prêtez-**les**-lui !	Lend them to him!
Vas-**y** !	Go on! *Literally: (Go to it!)*
Allez-**y** !	Go on!

Negative Commands revert to the normal pronoun order.

Ne	l'	écoute	pas !	Don't listen	to him!
Ne	les y	perdez	pas !	Don't lose	them there!

Pronouns with 2 Verbs

The pronouns go before the Verb of which they are the Object.

je vais	y	aller	I am going to go	there
tu ne veux pas	les	casser	you don't want to break	them
il va	les	punir	he is going to punish	them
nous voulons	les	inviter	we want to invite	them

Special structures/Idioms etc.

The following expressions are some of the most commonly used forms in French:

c'est p.84

il y a p.85

avoir 15 ans p.86

devoir p.87

il faut p.87

ça me plaît p.88

si p.88

depuis p.89

être p.90

venir de p.90

savoir/connaître p.90

Verbs with no preposition p.91

c'est = it is

This phrase is useful in conjunction with adjectives as a way of expressing an opinion. See page 59.

Présent	c'est	it is
	ce n'est pas	it isn't
	est-ce ?	is it?
	n'est-ce pas ?	isn't it?
(pluriel)	ce sont	they are
Passé composé	ça a été	it was (one off)
Imparfait	c'était	it was
Futur	ce sera	it will be
Conditionnel	ce serait	it would be

il y a = there is / there are

Présent	il y a	there is / there are
Passé composé	il y a eu	there was / there were
Imparfait	il y avait	there was / there were
Futur	il y aura	there will be
Conditionnel	il y aurait	there would be

Présent	il n'y a pas	there isn't there aren't
Passé composé	il n'y a pas eu	there wasn't (one off) there weren't (one off)
Imparfait	il n'y avait pas	there wasn't there weren't
Futur	il n'y aura pas	there won't be
Conditionnel	il n'y aurait pas	there wouldn't be

Présent	Il y a ? Y a-t-il ?	Is there? Are there?
Passé composé	Y a-t-il eu ?	Was there? (one off) Were there? (one off)
Imparfait	Y avait-il ?	Was there? Were there?
Futur	Y aura-t-il ?	Will there be?
Conditionnel	Y aurait-il ?	Would there be?

avoir = to have

In the following sentences avoir is translated am/are/is etc.

Quel âge **as**-tu ?	How old **are** you?
j'**ai** 15 ans	I **am** 15 (years old)
j'**ai** chaud	I **am** hot
j'**ai** froid	I **am** cold
j'**ai** faim	I **am** hungry
j'**ai** soif	I **am** thirsty
j'**ai** raison	I **am** right
j'**ai** tort	I **am** wrong
j'**ai** honte	I **am** ashamed
j'**ai** peur des araignées	I **am** afraid of spiders
j'**ai** sommeil	I **am** sleepy

j'**ai besoin** d'un couteau	I **need** (have need of) a knife

devoir = owe / must / to have to

je **dois** 10 euros à mon oncle	I **owe** my uncle 10 euros
je **dois** faire les courses	I **must** do the shopping
je **devrais** (conditional) rendre visite à mon grand-père	I **ought** to visit my granddad

il faut = it is necessary

This expression is used instead of *devoir* to have to to translate anything like **I need to**, **you must**, **they have to**, etc.

Infinitif	falloir	to be necessary
Présent	il faut	it is necessary
Passé Composé	il a fallu	it was necessary (one off)
Imparfait	il fallait	it was necessary / one had to
Futur proche *Immediate future (aller + infinitive)*	il va falloir	it is going to be necessary
Futur simple	il faudra	it will be necessary
Conditionnel	il faudrait	one should / one ought / it would be necessary

ça me plaît = (Literally) **that pleases me**

Commonly used in French to mean **"I like that"**

Infinitive: plaire = to please

Présent	ça me plaît	I like that
Passé composé	ça m'a plu	I liked it
Futur	ça me plaira	I shall like that
Conditionnel	ça me plairait	I would like that

Présent	ça ne me plaît pas	I don't like that
Passé composé	ça ne m'a pas plu	I didn't like it
Futur	ça ne me plaira pas	I shan't like that
Conditionnel	ça ne me plairait pas	I shouldn't like that

s'il te/vous plaît	Please (see page 7)

si = if

Si *If* je **vais** *I go (Présent)* à Londres, j'**irai** *I will go (Futur)* à l'abbaye de Westminster.

Si *If* je **gagnais** *I won/were to win (Imparfait)* la loterie, j'**achèterais** *I would buy (Conditionnel)* un château. *a castle.*

depuis = since

This idiom tells you for how long you have been doing something.

> The **PRESENT TENSE** is used for activities you have been doing for some time and **are still doing**.
> The **present tense** is used *precisely because* you **are still doing it**.

- If *you **are** still doing it*, the **Present** tense is used.

Présent *Present*

j'apprends *I have been learning* le français depuis *since/for* 4 ans *4 years*

j'attends *I have been waiting for* le bus depuis *for* une demi-heure *½ hour*

- If *you **were** still doing it*, the **Imperfect** is used.

Imparfait *Imperfect*

il regardait *he had been watching* le film depuis *for* 2 heures

on nageait *we had been swimming* dans la mer depuis *for* longtemps *a long time*

être = to be

je suis ^(I am) en train de ^(in the middle of) faire mes devoirs ^(doing my HW)

je suis ^(I'm) sur le point de ^(on the point of/about to) préparer le dîner ^(prepare the dinner)

venir de = (literally) to come from
= English idiom "to have just"

Présent:	je **viens de** ^(I have just) gagner un prix ^(won a prize)
Imparfait:	je **venais de** ^(I had just) marquer un but ^(scored a goal)

savoir = to know

je **sais** que les girafes sont grands
  I **know** that giraffes are tall **(FACT)**

je **sais** nager
  I **can** swim **(HAVE THE SKILL TO)**

connaître = to know a person or place

je ne **connais** pas le premier ministre
  I don't **know** the prime minister

reconnaître = to recognize

Verbs with a preposition in English but not in French

Be careful **not** to translate FOR, TO, AT with these 6 verbs:

attendre	wait FOR	il attend l'autobus
chercher	look FOR (seek)	je cherche mon ballon
demander	ask FOR	je lui demande un bonbon
écouter	listen TO	j'écoute la musique
payer	pay FOR	il a payé les billets
regarder	look AT	il regarde le professeur

Topic vocabulary

Les Numéros = Numbers

Even a small child can't get through life without knowing some numbers. The pronunciation of French numbers can cause confusion, so listen carefully to the video.

1	un / une	11	onze		
2	deux	12	douze		
3	trois	13	treize	30	trente
4	quatre	14	quatorze	40	quarante
5	cinq	15	quinze	50	cinquante
6	six	16	seize	60	soixante
7	sept	17	dix-sept		
8	huit	18	dix-huit		
9	neuf	19	dix-neuf		
10	dix	20	vingt		
		21	vingt et un		
		22	vingt-deux etc.		

93

From 70 onwards, the numbers are slightly complicated.

70	soixante-dix
71	soixante et onze
72	soixante-douze
73	soixante-treize

etc.

80	quatre-vingt**s**
81	quatre-vingt-un
82	-deux
83	-trois

etc.

90	quatre-vingt-dix
91	-onze
92	-douze
93	-treize
94	-quatorze
95	-quinze
96	-seize
97	-dix-sept
98	-dix-huit
99	-dix-neuf
100	cent

une diz*aine*	approx. 10
douz*aine*	= dozen
quinz*aine*	approx. 15
vingt*aine*	approx. 20
trent*aine*	approx. 30
quarant*aine*	approx. 40
cinquant*aine*	approx. 50
soixant*aine*	approx. 60
cent*aine*	approx. 100
mille	1,000
des milliers d'abeilles	thousands of bees
un million	1,000,000

Jours = days

The following words are all based on the word **jour** day

un **jour**	one day
le **jour**	the day
la **jour**née	the day (including activities)
bon**jour**	good morning / hello
bonne **jour**née	have a good day
au**jour**d'hui	today
tou**jours**	always
tous les **jours**	every day
le **jour**nal	the (daily) newspaper
le/la **jour**naliste	the journalist

Les Sept Jours Days de la Semaine Week

Sunday	**di**manche
Monday	lun**di**
Tuesday	mar**di**
Wednesday	mercre**di**
Thursday	jeu**di**
Friday	vendre**di**
Saturday	same**di**

Note:
- samedi — on Saturday
- le samedi — on Saturday**s**
- samedi dernier — last Saturday
- samedi prochain — next Saturday
- le weekend — (at) the weekend

Mois = months

Les Douze Mois ^Months de l'Année ^Year

janvier
février
mars
avril
mai
juin
juillet
août
septembre
octobre
novembre
décembre

> NB: No capital letters for days or months in French

Les Saisons (f) = The Seasons

au printemps	in spring
en été	in summer
en automne	in autumn
en hiver	in winter

L'Heure = hour/time

> **Quelle heure est-il ?**
> What's the time?

Il est *It's*   une heure   1 o'clock

deux heures

trois heures

midi   midday/noon

minuit   midnight

Il est *It's*   quatre heures **et quart**   quarter past 4

et demie   half past 4

5 heures **moins le quart**   quarter to 5

6 heures cinq   5 past 6

dix   10 past 6

etc.

La Météo = Weather (forecast)

> ## Quel temps fait-il ?
> What is the weather like?

il fait
- beau — fine
- mauvais — bad weather
- chaud — hot
- froid — cold
- de la brume — misty
- de l'orage — stormy
- des éclairs — lightning
- du brouillard — foggy
- du soleil — sunny
- du vent — windy
- nuageux — cloudy
- un temps couvert — grey / overcast

(faire — to do)

(un nuage — a cloud)

Tenses for Weather

Présent	il fait froid	it is cold
Passé composé	il a fait beau	it has been fine
Imparfait	il faisait du vent	it was windy
Futur	il fera du soleil	it will be sunny

D'autres ^{other} verbes pour la Météo

pleuvoir = to rain

Présent	il pleut	it is raining
Passé composé	il a plu	it has rained
Imparfait	il pleuvait	it was raining
Futur	il pleuvra	it will rain

Le soleil brille the sun is shining

il neige it's snowing (see page 17)

il gèle / il fait zéro degrés it's freezing

Les Villes = Towns

une <u>ville</u> = town

un <u>village</u> = village

à = to / at / in

Londres	London
Cantorbéry	Canterbury
Douvres	Dover
Edimbourg	Edinburgh
Paris	
Varsovie	Warsaw
Lyon	
Marseille	
Toulouse	
New York	
Toronto	

Les Pays = Countries

le pays = country   The **names** of most countries are feminine.

en (f) = to / in

Afrique	Africa (continent)
Allemagne	Germany
Amérique	America
Angleterre	England
Australie	Australia
Autriche	Austria
Belgique	Belgium
Chine	China
Corée	Korea
Ecosse	Scotland
Espagne	Spain
Europe	
France	
Grande-Bretagne	Great Britain
Hollande	Holland
Hongrie	Hungary
Inde	India
Irelande	Ireland
Islande	Iceland
Italie	Italy
Norvège	Norway
Nouvelle-Zélande	New Zealand
Pologne	Poland
Roumanie	Romania
Russie	Russia
Suède	Sweden
Suisse	Switzerland

au (m) = to / in

Canada	
Danemark	Denmark
Japon	Japan
Mexique	Mexico
Pakistan	
Pays-Bas	Low Countries / Netherlands
Pays de Galles	Wales
Portugal	
Royaume-Uni	UK

aux Etats-Unis USA

Le Vocabulaire du Sport

jouer = to play

- **au** badminton
- basket *basketball*
- football
- hockey
- golf
- ping-pong
- tennis
- rugby
- **à la** pétanque *bowls*
- **aux** échecs *chess*

faire = to do

- **du** sport
- cyclisme
- golf
- jogging
- judo
- patin à roulette *roller skating*
- patinage *skating*
- ski
- tir à l'arc *archery*
- vol libre *hang-gliding*
- VTT (vélo à tout terrain) *mountain biking*

de la danse
gymnastique
natation *swimming*
planche à voile *wind surfing*
voile *sailing*

de l' alpinisme *mountaineering*
athlétisme *athletics*
équitation *horse riding*
escalade *climbing*
escrime *fencing*

des randonnées (f) *rambles*
sports (m) de frisson *extreme sports*

D'autres *other* verbes pour le Sport

aller à la pêche *to go fishing*
aller à pied *to walk*
courir *to run*
danser *to dance*
faire une promenade *to go for a walk*
marcher *to walk*
nager *to swim* (see page 17)
promener le chien *to walk the dog* (see page 16)
* se balader *to stroll*
* se promener *to go for a walk* (see page 16)

* Reflexive. See page 25

La Musique = Music

jouer = to play

du
- basson ^{bassoon}
- clavier ^{keyboard}
- cor anglais ^{cor anglais}
- cor d'harmonie ^{French horn}
- hautbois ^{oboe}
- piano
- piccolo
- saxophone
- trombone
- violon ^{violin}
- violoncelle ^{'cello}

de la
- batterie ^{drum kit / drums}
- clarinette ^{clarinet}
- contrebasse ^{double bass}
- flûte ^{flute}
- guitare (électrique / basse) ^{(electric / bass) guitar}
- harpe ^{harp}
- trompette ^{trumpet}

des
- orgues (f) ^{church (or large) organ}

Vocabulary Tips

l'argent (m)	silver/money
la monnaie	(small) change

chaque	each
chac**un** (m)	each **one**
chac**une** (f)	each **one**

demain	tomorrow
après-**demain**	the day **after** tomorrow
le len**demain**	the next day
après	**after**
après-midi	**after**noon

près	near
presque	nearly

une chose	a thing
quelque chose	something

suivre	to follow (see page 24)
pour**sui**vre	to pursue
la **sui**te	cont. / next episode
en**sui**te	next
tout de **sui**te	immediately

la **cour**	playground/yard
la basse-**cour**	farmyard
le **cour**s / la leçon	lesson
le **cour**t de tennis	tennis court

ici here	**voi**ci here is
là there	**voi**là there is
là-bas over there	

une pièce	room (in a house)
une pièce (de 2 euros)	2€ coin
une pièce de théâtre	play
un morceau de fromage (m)	a piece of cheese

même	**same / even / self**
la **même** chose	the **same** thing
quand **même** / tout de **même**	all the **same**
même les petits	**even** little children
moi-**même**	my**self**
nous-**mêmes**	our**selves**

travailler	to work
voyager	to travel
le voyage	journey
la journée	day

	porter	to carry
	apporter	to bring (eg: du vin)
	ra**p**porter	to bring back
	emporter	to take away
	remporter une mèdaille	to carry off a medal
	mener	to lead (eg: a person/animal)
	amener	to bring (eg: un ami)
	ramener	to bring back
	emmener	to lead/take away

à pied, en courant = walking, running

je vais au stade à pied	I walk to the stadium
je suis allé au cinéma à pied	I walked to the cinema
je suis venu à pied	I walked here
je suis allé au parc en courant	I ran to the park
je suis venu en courant	I ran here

à vélo = by bike

je suis allé à la forêt à vélo	I cycled to the forest

Visiting and meeting

visiter to visit	les musées
	Londres
	Paris
	la cathédrale
	la France
	l'Angleterre
rendre visite à to pay a visit to	ma famille
	mes cousins
	ma grand-mère
	mon grand-père

Rencontrer	to encounter, meet, bump into
Rejoindre	to meet up with, join

J'ai rejoint *I met up with* mes copains *my friends*

Rendez-vous *Meet (verb)* devant la gare ! *outside the station!*

J'ai *I have* **rendez-vous** *an appointment (noun)* chez le dentiste *at the dentist's*

Leaving and returning (Use the right verb!)

LEAVE	a place or someone	quitter	il a quitté la maison
		partir	il faut partir (NB: this verb has no object)
	a thing behind	laisser	j'ai laissé mon livre
RETURN	= go **home**	**re**ntrer	il est rentré à six heures
	= come **back**	**re**venir	il va revenir en Angleterre
	= GO **back**	**re**tourner	il est retourné au magasin
	= GIVE **back**	**re**ndre	il a rendu le livre à son ami

s'amuser = to enjoy yourself
to have a good time
to have fun

Do NOT attempt to translate the English literally

je m'amuse bien chez moi	I enjoy myself at home
je ne m'amuse pas bien chez mes cousins	I don't have a good time at my cousins' house
je me suis très bien amusé(e) dans mon cours de français	I had great fun in my French lesson
je ne me suis pas du tout bien amusé(e) au collège ce matin	I didn't enjoy myself at all at school this morning

The End – La Fin

Acknowledgements

I am deeply grateful to our son, John, who has laboured countless hours on word-processing this book and the Workbook. As a teacher himself, he has also made numerous useful suggestions to make everything as clear as possible to the students.

Printed in Great Britain
by Amazon